How to Sta

By: Brian James

Table of Contents

Chapter 6: Cleaning Quiz (50 Questions)

Introduction

You are entrepreneurial minded but lack two key things: business experience and capital. You may not have a business idea yet, but "working for the man" is not in your future. Starting a home cleaning service is a great launching pad for the entrepreneur: with a minimal initial investment ($300 or less), you can turn serious profit fast (without going into debt) and use this income to fund your passions. Or, build up the business and enjoy financial stability for years to come.

Why residential cleaning?

- Ease of entry because of highly fragmented industry. This means there is no single company that dominates the cleaning market. In fact, most homeowners prefer a boutique cleaning service over a local franchise; even better, they are willing to pay a premium for it.

- High profit margins (the biggest cost is labor, which can be absorbed by performing the work yourself…at least in the beginning).

- Low overhead (there is no need for an office or storefront. Run a lucrative and always-in-demand business from the internet and your vehicle).

- Create awesome connections in your local area that will greatly expand your current network of contacts.

- Set your own rates (charge $30+ per hour).

- Recession-proof: when economic times are good,

people can afford cleaning as a luxury. When times are tough, there are more dual-working households, and outside cleaning help becomes a necessity for many.

On the job…

- Set your own hours.
- Listen to music or enrich your mind through podcasts.
- Burn calories.
- Learn entrepreneurial skills that will serve you down the road, from online marketing to vendor sourcing and accounting.

This book is designed to give you *specific* steps to launch your business in under a month. The first section outlines different administrative tasks to complete, the second section examines some inexpensive (often times free) ways to market your cleaning service, the third section explores operations, and the final section offers cleaning tutorials, miscellaneous tips and a cleaning quiz.

The traditional way to build a cleaning business is by first performing the cleaning yourself, and slowly transitioning to a hands-off, managerial role once you have enough business coming in to sustain a cleaning crew. Or, you can decide *not* to scale the business if you are content with the headache-free lifestyle a solo operation provides.

If you decide to scale the business beyond yourself, your role goes from cleaner to acquiring new customers, quality control, payroll, hiring, firing, etc. This can be an extremely lucrative route over time if you can stomach the industry's high employee turnover rate, workers showing up late, customer complaints, and other challenges that come with leading a team. The upside is that you can operate a profitable business for years without worrying about becoming physically burnt out, and your earning potential is unlimited. Eventually, after years of hard work, the opportunity to sell your book of business for a large sum of money may come about. In any case, it is wise to start solo.

The solo (owner-operator) model involves you conducting the cleaning yourself. It requires substantial physical work on your behalf, and is difficult to scale (one worker can only handle so much; thus, you are limited as to how much you can earn). However, administrative headaches are reduced significantly: payroll is simplified, you have complete control over the quality of work, and profit margins are extremely high. You can charge $50/an hour, work three hours, and net around $100 after all expenses are paid. These are great margins. The best part is you will generate cash flow immediately for your business without going into debt. Leverage this window of time to save as much cash as possible. Your cash reserve will help fund your expansion into hiring employees (should you decide to go in this direction) down the road.

You may experience burnout quickly, however, if

trying to tackle too high of a workload. I recommend cleaning no more than two small homes a day—or one large home—if you are the sole employee of your business. Other drawbacks include flexibility: if you choose to go on vacation, your business stops. If you sustain an injury, your business stops. It is a wise idea to have contingency plans in place incase this happens (like partnering with another cleaning professional in your area to take over these accounts in your absence). The good news is that you have complete authority over your business and its image.

Again, the most common way to build a cleaning business is by initially performing the cleaning yourself, and slowly transitioning to a management role once you have enough business coming in to sustain a cleaning crew (or continue your solo operation). This guide will help you get to this transition point.

Chapter 1: Administrative "To Do's"

Take time in the beginning to lay a solid foundation for your cleaning business. It may be tempting to cut corners in the administrative area to cut costs. Remember, however, that the more legitimate you make your business from the start, the faster you will earn customers' trust (especially in regards to carrying liability insurance).

First, choose a business name for your cleaning service. Check to make sure the chosen name is not taken by performing a search on your Secretary of State's website. Keep in mind your target market, and choose a name accordingly. This can be your own name for a more personal approach (i.e. Sally's Cleaning), or a more impersonal name if your goal is to build the business well beyond yourself (i.e. Champion Cleaning) Keep it short and sweet, and related to your cleaning niche if you have one (Sally's Rental Cleaning). You can always change your business name at a later date as your business evolves.

Tip: Businesses starting with the letter "A" have the advantage of appearing at the beginning of most business listing directories.

Once you have decided on a business name, it is time to let your local and state officials know that you are starting a business.

A. Business Registration and Licensing

1. Set up your limited liability company (LLC) by filing an "Articles of Organization" form found

on your state's business website ($50 to $150). Or, use legalzoom.com. This will help protect your personal assets in the event of a lawsuit.

2. Once your new business request is processed, apply for an Employer Identification Number (EIN) with the IRS (apply online).

3. Once you receive your EIN, use this to set up a business checking account at your local bank.

4. Buy a state vendor's license. This allows you to charge and withhold sales tax in the county you will do business in ($25-50). This can be completed online in most states.

5. Check with your city and state to see if there is any other registration or licensing requirements.

6. Link your newly formed business checking account to Wave Accounting, a free accounting software (www.waveapps.com). This will automatically track expenditures and income.

7. Sign up for a free Paypal account to accept credit cards online (www.paypal.com).

8. Shop around for basic business liability insurance ($250-600 annually, depending on coverage).

9. Read and obtain a basic understanding of federal, state, and city tax code for your business. It can be overwhelming, but don't fret. You need only have a *basic* grasp of your tax obligations when you keep good financial records and outsource all accounting and payroll services.

- I recommend finding an accountant (another option is using TurboTax Business, software that allows you to self-prepare your tax returns).
- Ask your accountant about filing for "S-corp" status to save on taxes once your LLC is formed.
- Remember to keep careful track of your income and expenses. Keep your personal and business expenses separate.
- Be sure to save all receipts. Your accountant is unable to complete a proper year-end tax return with sloppy record keeping. Other services, such as the free app Shoeboxed, allow you to take pictures and store your receipts digitally.

*This list is not all-inclusive. Refer to federal, state and local regulatory guidelines to ensure you have proper licensing, business registration and tax requirements taken care of for your cleaning business.

B. Booking

Scheduling cleaning customers strategically may not seem like an urgent matter at first, but as business picks up, it is absolutely critical that you minimize driving time between customers to ensure maximum cleaning time and help curb expenses. Fuel costs can be a huge expense for cleaning services, and being mindful of these numbers will motivate you to shorten the distance between customers when scheduling—a major player in your bottom line. When an employee of yours must drive 40 minutes to and from a client's home, precious time is ticking that could be spent cleaning. Schedule customers geographically and carefully track business fuel expenses and miles driven for tax purposes. Mile IQ is a handy mileage tracking app for your phone that uses GPS to automatically calculate miles driven: www.mileiq.com. **Most business related vehicle costs are tax deductible. Save your receipts!** To help concentrate customers in one area, utilize the power of neighbor referrals. This helps build trust, too: would-be clients are more likely to trust a cleaning company if their neighbors are using the same service. This creates a sense of community around your cleaning service that helps sales surge.

As far as the process of booking is concerned, online booking can be a nice add-on to your cleaning business website. Even if customers do not use this tool on your site, it creates perceived value. Most online scheduling software even sends appointment reminders and confirmation emails to your customers. Usually this involves simply plugging in your availability, blocking off days/times you are busy, and copy/pasting html code from the scheduling software onto your website (a very easy maneuver that involves just a bit of computer savvy and no coding whatsoever). We recommend www.AcuityScheduling.com, a site that offers free and paid versions of their software. Another *excellent* option is PocketSuite (www.pocketsuite.io). PocketSuite is an app that provides online scheduling, payment, messaging and automatic appointment reminders for you and your customers. It has a free and paid version of their software, low processing rates, and frequent improvements. Customers have the option to tip, which is particularly valuable for one-time jobs (when they are more likely to tip). PocketSuite can be setup with only a smartphone. It involves no coding.

Note: Keeping your availability up-to-date can be time consuming. If you aren't tech-savvy, stay away from adding online booking to your site.

C. Pricing Work

Method #1: Hourly Rate (recommended)

Home cleaning involves many variables that make estimating time spent at a particular job difficult. A small, cramped home may take longer to clean than a larger home. Ensure you are getting paid for your time by charging an hourly rate. Your hourly rate should account for overhead (including taxes, insurance, supplies, etc.) and profit.

Calculating your hourly rate takes some number crunching, so get out those calculators. For simplicity's sake, we will assume that you are the only worker.

1. Determine what you want your salary to be after taxes. For this example, let's assume 50k.

2. Add 15% to cover taxes (payroll taxes, federal, etc.) Now we have $57,500.

3. Project monthly overhead (utilities, cleaning supplies, advertising/marketing, insurance, etc.) Let's say this figure is $500 per month. Multiply this by 12, and we have $6,000.

4. Calculate your annual billable hours. Assuming you work 51 weeks a year (1 week vacation), 40 hours a week, we arrive at 2,040 hours worked.

5. Add items 2 and 3 together (salary + 15% + overhead). Now, we have $63,500. $63,500 divided by 2,040 billable hours is $31/hour.

6. Now, factor in your profit margin. A healthy profit margin is absolutely essential for your business's success over time. Let's go with 15%. 15% times $31 is $4.65. Your final hourly rate, after rounding down, is $35/hour! ($31 + $4).

7. If you add another worker, simply charge your hourly rate per worker per hour. Adjust your hourly rate as necessary to remain competitive in your area.

If you think $35/worker/hour is too high, think again. A legitimate, above-board business will not survive charging cheap rates. You must account for growth, taxes, and other fixed and unforeseen expenses. Also, higher prices provide some cushion for you to provide discounts without totally eating your margins.

Tip #1: Customers need estimates for given jobs, not just your hourly rate. Create a pricing chart for your website (like the one outlined in "Method #2") that uses your hourly rate to estimate how much a house will cost to clean based on its size. An estimated pricing chart is helpful so people know your ballpark end price without having to guess the number of hours their house will take to clean. Stress on your website that these are estimated prices, not fixed rates. In other words, you can quote potential clients using these figures, but ultimately use your hourly rate to determine final cost. Make sure you get approval of a customer before going over the quoted prices.

Tip #2: Consider offering a 5-10% discount to clients who sign up for reoccurring service.

Method #2: Fixed Pricing

Fixed pricing, while not recommended, has its benefits. It takes the guesswork out of estimates, and offers clear, simple pricing for the customer. Fixed pricing is often determined by square footage, # of bathrooms, # of bedrooms, or a combination thereof.

This method is helpful for quoting customers who are interested in reoccurring service. For big, one-time deep cleanings (especially move-in/out), strictly use an hourly rate to protect yourself from under pricing your work.

Here is an example of fixed pricing:

Note that these figures are *before* sales tax. All supplies included.

1 Bedroom

$109

2 Bedrooms

$129

3 Bedrooms

$149

4 Bedrooms

$169

Note: Each estimate above includes up to 2 full bathrooms, 1 half bathroom, 1 living room, 1 dining room and 1 spare room (i.e. den) in addition to the bedrooms. Extra full bathrooms are $10 each, extra half bathrooms and spare rooms are $5 each.

Extras:

Inside Oven

$20

Inside Fridge

$20

Inside Cabinets

$30

Interior Windows:

$40

Baseboards:

$20

Blinds (washing):

Tip #1: While it may be tempting to help drum up new business, avoid under-pricing work during your launch. This helps in terms of image and provides cushion for growth.

Tip #2: It can be difficult to accurately quote customers prior to seeing their home, especially for an initial deep cleaning. For the first visit, I recommend requesting payment in the form of check after the work is completed, rather than asking for payment upfront. This initial cleaning will help you price subsequent cleanings down the road. If you are worried about not getting paid, request a $200 deposit upfront, and bill the difference later.

D. Invoicing

There are a host of equally viable options for sending invoices to customers for your cleaning services. The three primary options are cash, check and electronic billing.

There are both pros and cons to electronic invoicing, such as PayPal:

Pros	Cons
-Easy and convenient for customers	-Merchant fees apply (and add up!)
-Easily organize customer information	-Billing after the work is completed runs the risk of

	non-payment
-Export transactions to an Excel spreadsheet for easy accounting	-Customer billing information may be vulnerable to cyber-attacks
-Record customer email addresses for newsletter use, appointment reminders, etc.	

Check out the following online payment services to determine the best fit for your business:

www.Square.com

www.PayPal.com

www.PocketSuite.io (recommended)

Tip: Online billing usually means the customer pays after *the work is completed. This comes with inherent risk of nonpayment. To mitigate this risk, request check or cash payment for new customers. Once trust is built, offer them the convenience of paying online.*

Chapter 2: The Spark (Marketing)

Here is the beautiful thing about home cleaning: you can build up a highly successful cleaning service with little to no marketing. Word of mouth is powerful, especially if you provide a truly valuable service and you actively let customers know you are seeking new business.

Start with friends and family in your area. Tell them you are starting a cleaning business. Once you iron out the kinks of your operation, friends and family can help propel the first wave of customer referrals.

A. Referral Discount

Encourage referrals by offering a $20 discount on current customers' next cleaning. This is a great way to grow a loyal network of clients and make known your intention to grow your business.

Benefits include:

- Geographical concentration (neighbors telling neighbors)
- Scheduling flexibility (I have had several instances where two clients communicate independent of me to "swap" days during a certain week, saving me administrative time).
- People love the extra sense of security referrals offer. Customers who hire you through referrals are already "broken in," so to speak, and are more willing to trust you with keys to the house.

At this time, begin setting up your web presence.

B. Website

1. Choose a website builder. I recommend using either www.wix.com or www.squarespace.com to design your website. This will cost around $100 annually. Or, design one for free at 000WebHost.com. No coding skills are required—each platform uses simple drag-and-drop technology and handles your website's hosting.

   Add your website's content (services, prices, etc.) and you are good to go.

2. Buy a domain name (cleaningsite.com) through the hosting site (above) or through www.GoDaddy.com. This will be $10-$20 a year.

3. Register your business with online business registries and review websites:

   - Google (and Bing) Local Business Listings (show up organically in a web search when prospective customers search "home cleaning" in your area).

   - www.Yelp.com (expect a tremendous response from yelp.com once a few positive reviews are posted, particularly considering the importance of character and reputation in residential cleaning. I had to contact the website at one point to have my business removed as I could not keep up with demand!).

   - www.Manta.com is a free business listing platform that offers free daily tips and insights to help keep your marketing strategies up-to-date.

Once you have your web foundation in place, add a few tweaks to ensure optimum performance of your website.

C. Free Estimate

Create an estimate request form on your website through www.form2go.com or www.wufoo.com, free form building websites.

A *functional* website is pivotal in converting new business online. Aside from listing your phone number and email on your website, an online form is appealing to an increasingly tech-savvy prospect, and it gives you a chance to look at your calendar and formulate a thoughtful and cleanly articulated response before getting back to the customer. Also, this is a great opportunity to collect emails for your online newsletter, which we will get to later. Be sure to ask customers if they would like to "opt-in" before adding them to your email list.

How it works: using the form building websites listed above, create a questionnaire collecting customer contact information. Create the following question fields:

What city and state do you live in?

What is the square footage of your home?

Number of bathrooms?

Number of bedrooms?

What frequency of cleaning do you need?

Do you have any specific requests?

Would you like to receive our free monthly newsletter?

Once completed, add the form to your website by copying the HTML generated by the form building website to your site (this part is not as difficult as it seems—follow the instructions at www.form2go.com or www.wufoo.com). After a potential customer fills out the form on your site, an automated email response is sent thanking them for the inquiry and telling them you will respond shortly. Coming home after a day of work to an inbox of multiple estimate requests is a rewarding feeling, but you had better not wait too long to respond: precious time is ticking for other cleaning services to come into the picture.

Tip #1: To mitigate the risk of under-quoting a job, add a disclaimer on the form itself stating you have the right to adjust the estimate after seeing the job in person.

Tip #2: Create an optional "home address" field, and use a third party real estate platform (i.e. Zillow, Trulia) to visually aid your estimate.

Name (required)

Email (required)

City, State

I am interested in: (required)

home cleaning

 # Bathrooms

0

 # Bedrooms

0

Frequency

Once

Please specify, if needed

Submit »

D. Online Newsletter

Create an online newsletter and announce your launch. Distribute it freely among family, friends, former teachers or professors—any contact you may have. Scan your email contacts, facebook and linked-in and make a list of every email you deem relevant. Remember—everyone needs cleaning! (Use www.mailchimp.com).

A monthly newsletter allows you to express specific changes and promotions in front of a targeted audience month to month. Everyone loves following the growth of a well-intentioned startup. Include useful general information too (not specific to your business) to keep non-customers subscribed—I added one or two handy cleaning tips per newsletter that received great feedback. The free Mailchimp platform allows you to track every newsletter's performance, providing real time statistics on the number of clicks, who opened your email, and any resulting action (i.e. how many people clicked on the gift certificate link you included). See sample emails below.

Benefits include:

- Ability to stay in front of your audience monthly

- Creatively articulate the changing landscape of your startup (did you hire a new cleaner? Introduce him or her here!)

- Communicate promotions and holiday specials with functional links to your website and even PayPal.

- Establish in the eyes of your local audience that you indeed are the cleaning expert (the internet is filled with free cleaning tips and methods that you can relay to your customers).

Note: to comply with anti-spam laws, ensure all email contacts have given you written consent to send them your newsletter. Make sure your physical address is visibly located at the bottom of all marketing emails, as well as an "unsubscribe" option.

Add a "subscribe" section on your website where email addresses are collected. Also, generate a terms and conditions page on your website stating that use of your website, including any payments made via PayPal, implies consent to receive marketing emails from you in the future. A long list of legitimate email contacts will prove invaluable to your marketing efforts down the road. Include seasonal discounts, introduce new workers, and give free cleaning tips in your newsletter.

Examples:

immersion
HOME CLEANING

Hi << Test First Name >>,

It's hard to believe 2012 is coming to a close already. Thanks to everyone who has helped support my new business venture.

Now, your support also helps make the lives of two local breast cancer patients a little more bearable. Im excited to announce a new partnership with Cleaning For A Reason--a non-profit connecting cleaning services and local breast cancer patients.

Immersion Home Cleaning will pledge two free cleanings per month. So, if you know anyone in the Cleveland area undergoing treatment for breast cancer, I encourage you to give them my contact information.

On another note, I hope you enjoy December's cleaning tip. And, if you are in a crunch when it comes to finding the perfect gift for your sister, mother, etc--you can now purchase a cleaning gift certificate here!

Have a nice holiday,

Brian

immersion
HOME CLEANING

<< Test First Name >>,

I've taken my Immersion Home Cleaning system to the next level of quality.

Current customers, rejoice: I will now be spinning from baseboard to baseboard, juking out your dog while I wash every square inch of your floors *by hand*--reaching a new level of immersion. Goodbye mop and bucket.

How? I'll show you:

These are heavy duty knee pads on wheels, called Knee Blades. The wheels are specially designed for safe use on any hardwood or tile surface (mark-free), making hand-washing floors both painless and efficient.

So, after zapping dust, hair and dirt with this...

...floors are now 100% hand-washed for the deepest clean possible.

E. Cause Marketing

Cause-marketing is powerful—don't be discouraged by the prospect of giving away free work early on. Charities often seek the donations of local businesses to help fulfill raffle prizes and raise money from other donors. In turn, these businesses are listed as event sponsors in the event's promotional materials.

I joined Cleaning for A Reason, a non-profit providing two free cleanings a month to local breast cancer patients. Partnering with this program not only gave me great fulfillment in helping patients undergoing chemotherapy, it indirectly generated close to $5,000 in new business simply because of my business' affiliation with the program. Family and friends who see you give to their loved ones are anxious to help propel your own success. It's a win-win.

F. Networking

Introduce yourself to as many realtors and real estate agencies in your service area as you can. They need your services before putting a client's dirty home on the market, or before letting their client move into a dirty home. Move-in/out and presale cleanings are highly lucrative if priced properly (homeowners are willing to pay a premium if it speeds up the sale of their home). Contact listing agents in your area and introduce yourself—realtors can be a source of endless, qualified leads. You can carve about an awesome niche in this area! An added bonus is that these properties are often times completely vacant and free of furniture.

In addition to networking with realtors, landlords and property managers can use your services as well for tenant turnovers. These gigs can be challenging, but can pay very well (especially if the property is in shambles), even in the thousands. It is wise to see the property first before accepting this type of job—some may require removing trash, etc. and dumpster rental prior to cleaning. You may or may not want to accept large projects such as this depending on the size of your crew and your experience level. You can always outsource jobs you do not feel comfortable completing yourself to other reputable companies in your area, which we will explore later.

If you find yourself drawn to the idea of tenant turnovers, connect with your area's Airbnb.com community of hosts. Airbnb is a peer-to-peer house rental company. Owners of these properties desperately need quality cleaning services to turn their properties over in timely fashion before their next guest arrives. Some Airbnb property owners rent their homes (or condos) several times a month, providing you with an opportunity to negotiate a contract with them.

Look up the phone numbers and email addresses of realtors and landlords in your area and start dialing, and follow up via LinkedIn. You will quickly have more work than you can handle!

Summary

1. Create website with www.wix.com, www.squarespace.com or for free at 000WebHost.

2. Hang pull-tab flyers in apartment complexes and community boards at coffee shops.

3. Create an introductory newsletter announcing your launch, and distribute it freely amongst family, friends, professors—any contact you may have. Scan your email contacts, facebook and linked-in and make a list of every email you deem relevant. Remember—everyone needs cleaning! (Use www.mailchimp.com).

4. Network with local real estate agents and agencies.

5. Join Cleaning for A Reason.

6. Register your business with a handful of free online platforms: Manta.com, Yelp.com, Google.com

7. Encourage referrals by offering a finder's fee to customers.

Before going all-in, review some of the pros and cons of residential cleaning versus commercial cleaning, and the pros and cons of starting a cleaning business from starch versus buying a franchise.

Why residential?

Pros:

- High profit margins (the main cost is labor).

- Low running overhead (no storefront needed, no taking out crippling loans)

- Positive cash flow (expect to be paid immediately, or soon after, the work is completed).

- The home cleaning industry is highly fragmented. This means great ease of entry. While commercial cleaning is cost driven, with lowest bidders often winning contracts, residential cleaning involves a component of trust that homeowners are often willing to pay a premium for. It actually helps, in many cases, to be the small mom and pop rather than the franchise.

Cons:

- Residential cleaning involves workers coming into contact with sensitive areas of a customer's home. Jewelry, money, prescription pills, etc. are often times out in the open. As a cleaning service owner, you must take measures to ensure your workers (if you have any) are trustworthy and have no criminal record.

- Private house cleaning jobs require a more thorough cleaning than most janitorial work. Expect customers to nit-pick a bit more than, say, the tenants of an office building. Every homeowner has their quirks, and it is your job to cater towards them.

- Working in tight spaces surrounded by valuable objects raises the possibility of you or your crew causing damage.

Why commercial?

Pros:

- While the margins are a bit lower and pricing is more competitive, commercial (janitorial) work provides an excellent platform to build up a large cleaning empire. You are dealing with much larger numbers in commercial cleaning, and when priced right, the opportunity to realize serious profits is undoubtedly there.

- The impersonal working environment of most commercial spaces makes it much easier to delegate work. The risk of theft and damage is greatly diminished compared to residential cleaning.

Cons:

- Because of tight margins in commercial cleaning, a larger volume of accounts is required before seeing a profit.

- The commercial cleaning industry is driven primarily by cost. Reputation is still important, but expect the "new guy" to come in and attempt to undercut your price to take over your account.

- Because of the size of most commercial accounts, more manpower is required. Expect high turnover, high labor costs and more administrative work than residential cleaning services encounter.

- Cash flow problems: most commercial cleaning companies are paid with net 30 (or 60) terms, meaning payment is due 30 days after an invoice for a particular month is received. Workers, however, are paid (usually) every two weeks. Commercial cleaning services must ensure they have enough cash on hand to pay their workers while waiting to receive payments from large accounts.

Starting a cleaning business from scratch:

Pros:

- Creative agency (*you* call all the shots, from branding and marketing to determining the best method to clean a toilet).

- No royalty or large franchise fee (leverage the low-cost entry into the cleaning industry by starting from scratch and seeing a return in under a month).

Cons:

- Without the aid of a nationally recognized brand, some leg work is required before landing those first few customers.

- There is no proven business plan/blueprint to follow; you must create your own way through trial and error.

Buying a cleaning franchise:

Pros:

- The franchisee is provided with a proven business model and other forms of educational/business support.

- Most franchises offer marketing support and national brand recognition.

Cons:

- A large amount of capital is required to purchase a franchise

- Ongoing royalty fees are standard (and usually fall between %5-%10 of gross revenue).

- Creative agency is restricted for franchisees.

Chapter 3: Operations

A. Clean Image

With thousands of home cleaning companies out there, it pays to invest in the clean image of your service. A clean, professional image will evoke trust and stability in the eyes of your customers. This includes having cleaning uniforms, a clean vehicle with decals, freshly shaven faces, properly kept cleaning equipment, and more.

Here are some tips to help your cleaning service achieve the cleanest, most professional image possible:

- **Clean out your cleaning caddy *daily*.** After each day on the job, expect your cleaning caddy to be sufficiently dirty from spilled chemicals, excess moisture and dirt. Nothing is more of a put-off for a customer than cleaners entering their home with dirty cleaning supplies.

- **Clean your vacuum weekly.** This will help sterilize your equipment, prevent foul odors from contaminating carpets, and ensure maximum cleaning performance for years to come.

- **Keep your company vehicle clean.** The cleanliness of your car is a direct reflection of your business's professionalism. A dirty car will suggest a slapdash operation to customers and passerbys. If you are serious about growing your cleaning business beyond yourself, consider investing in marketing decals for your vehicle, whether vinyl decals or magnetic signs purchased through www.vistaprint.com.

- **Invest in company uniforms.** Design a company t-shirt in no time using www.vistaprint.com. Plan to buy two shirts per employee to ensure clean garments throughout the work week. You do not need to purchase premium uniforms; a simple t-shirt or polo with your logo (there is no need to invest in an expensive logo. For $5, a quality graphic designer will design your logo at www.fiverr.com!)

- **Design quality business cards for your cleaning service.** This step is absolutely necessary, and couldn't be easier using (again) www.vistaprint.com. Simply upload your logo, and fill in your contact details and service offerings. Buy 500-1000 cards to begin, and distribute them generously to customers. Give each customer 10+ business cards, and encourage them to give friends and family your information.

B. Subcontracting

When starting your cleaning business, don't try to be a "jack-of-all-trades" when it comes to services you offer. Specialize in a niche, and strive to be the best in your area at it. My niche in the home cleaning industry happened to be rental turnovers and move-in/out cleaning—large jobs that tended to be high paying. However, this doesn't mean you have to completely ignore the tremendous opportunity to cash in on extra cleaning services such as window cleaning, carpet cleaning, flood restoration, and more. Best of all, you do not need to physically complete these tasks yourself. Find reputable companies in your area who offer these services, and subcontract specialized projects to them.

As a contractor, charge your customer the cost of hiring your subcontractor plus a small markup, such as 10%. This convenience fee is commonplace, and all parties win (typically): your customer doesn't have to chase down several companies to have reputable work completed, your subcontractor charges their normal rates, and you make a small percentage for simply arranging the work to be completed. Furthermore, the more connections you make with potential subcontractors, the better: these companies will return the favor and refer you to their customers as the "go-to" cleaning company in your particular niche.

Add-on services to be subcontracted include (but are not limited to):

- Carpet cleaning
- Window cleaning
- Gutter cleaning
- Powerwashing
- Stripping/waxing floors
- Painting (interior and exterior)

- Fire/flood restoration

Tip: before you subcontract cleaning services, be sure to check with potential subcontractors to confirm they carry worker's comp, as well as basic liability insurance. Request copies of both before letting these providers into the home's of your customers.

1. Get quotes from each contractor, mark up a small percentage (i.e. 5-10%) and get work approval from property owner.

2. Pay contractors directly after invoicing property owner for total work amount.

C. Cleaning Supplies and Equipment

Create a business vendor account at a local supply store to receive discounts on future purchases. Purchase the following items (or their generic brands):

Cleaning Products	Function
Baking soda	Toilet bowls, bathtub/stall scrubbing
Windex	Mirrors and windows
Lemon Pledge	Stainless steel appliances, granite countertops, leather/finished wood furniture
White vinegar (5% acidity)	Sink deodorization, wood floor cleaning (1/4 cup vinegar: 1 gallon water).

	Avoid use on natural stone as erosion/dulling may occur.
All-purpose cleaner	Kitchen/bathroom surfaces.
Bathroom cleaner/soap scum remover	Toilets, sinks, bathtub/shower stall

Note: If you are unsure of using a cleaning product on a certain surface, test a small amount in an unnoticeable area.

Cleaning Tools	Function
Mr. Clean Magic Eraser (or generic)	Remove scuff marks on doors and walls. Scrub shower doors (then squeegee) without scratching glass. Chemical-free soap scum remover for shower, bath and sink.
Scrubbing/scouring pad	For use on stubborn mold, mildew and soap scum buildup. Be careful of scratching surfaces.
Microfiber cloths	Used to dust delicate furniture, countertops, mirrors, etc. Avoid using bleach to wash microfiber cloths.

Toilet brush	Used to scrub toilet bowl.
Scrubbing brush	Use on grout
12" squeegee	Remove excess water from shower doors, windows and mirrors.
Standard mop	Use on tile floor.
Damp mop (with microfiber pad)	Use on wood floor (also laminate, etc.)
Upright or canister vacuum cleaner	Use on carpet/hard floors.
Backpack vacuum* with brush attachment	Use on hard floors, baseboards and furniture.
Feather duster	Used to dust furniture, ceiling fans, blinds

* Why buy a backpack vacuum cleaner?

Having serviced homes, apartments and commercial buildings over 1,000 times the past several years, there is one tool that single-handily changed the trajectory of my cleaning business: the backpack vacuum cleaner. If a home is mostly hard floors, this vacuum outperforms both canister and upright vacuums. It can tough to maneuver in tight spaces, however, so use caution.

Efficiency, efficiency, efficiency. The backpack vacuum:

- Allows long-duration cleaning without continuously changing outlets

- Provides non-obstructed cleaning power to hard-to-reach areas (under tables, chairs, ceiling vents, upholstery, etc.)

- Has incredible suction for years (little to no maintenance, too: no clogged brush-rollers or broken belts)

If you do have carpeted areas you wish to clean with your backpack vacuum, consider purchasing a power-nozzle. This attachment uses the backpack vacuum cleaner's powerful suction to propel its rotating brush. If a home is mostly carpet with only some hard floors, a canister vacuum is your best option. Over time, it is helpful to have a backpack vacuum and a canister vacuum. This way, they can serve as each others' backup and you can clean any home optimally.

Tips:

1. Start building business credit and earn cash back by opening a card at the time of your first major purchase (i.e. new vacuum cleaner).

2. Buy cleaning product concentrates whenever possible.

3. If you provide cleaning rags, consider washing them in bulk at a laundry mat to save on your water bill and reducing wear and tear to your washer and dryer. This may help save you time by not having to clean towels every night.

4. Keep all receipts and record all equipment and supplies purchases.

5. If you use Magic Erasers as your primary bathroom scrubber (recommended), consider buying generic erasers from www.Aliexpress.com for pennies on the dollar. While the quality of these erasers are not as durable as brand names, they are truly disposable, and can be thrown out after each use at a customer's home without breaking the bank. *Expect to buy 100 magic erasers for around $5.*

D. Cleaning

Upon arrival, customer will greet you (or let yourself in if you've already been given instructions).

Do a quick walk-through of house so that...

- you can spot any curveballs (significant dirtiness, pet messes, etc).
- job timing and main areas of focus can be planned out.
- you can scan surfaces and identify needed cleaning agents.

Begin with the kitchen and bathrooms first, as they are often the most time consuming areas to clean.

1. Bathroom(s)

- Clean accessible vents with a damp corner of a towel.
- Wipe light fixtures (use caution) with damp towel.
- Spot clean tile walls with damp magic eraser and water. Wipe clean.

- Dry dust lightly soiled blinds with soft cloth. Wash soiled blinds using a drop of dishsoap in warm water. Wipe clean.

- Clean mirror and counters (Windex and soft cloth). Spray solution on counters and let sit for a minute while cleaning mirrors. Clean and buff counters to a clean, non-slippery finish.

- Clean shower door with magic eraser or scratch-free sponge and an all-purpose bathroom cleaner. After wetting the eraser/sponge with bathroom cleaner (and water), buff shower glass in circular motion. Squeegee the soapy solution down the shower door to the floor. Re-wet eraser and scrub shower and bathtub surfaces, as well as fixtures. Wipe clean. (*Note: if excess soap scum is built up on tub walls and shower interior, apply a thin layer of Softscrub Bleach. Do not let bleach come into contact with faucet fixtures). Scrub and wipe clean.

- Clean natural stone shower stalls with ¼ cup stone cleaner concentrate and ½ gallon warm water.

- Clean sink and faucet fixtures with magic eraser or the non-abrasive side of a scratch-free sponge. Wipe clean.

- Clean base, back and top of toilet (wear gloves and use all-purpose and rag). Wad up a small amount of toilet paper and wipe underneath the toilet lid and rim. Discard and flush. Then, clean toilet bowl with toilet cleaner (or half-cup white vinegar) and scrubber. To finish, buff dry all exposed porcelain on toilet with a rag. It should feel completely dry to the touch. Replace toilet paper as needed. For an added touch, put a drop of lavender essential oil on the inside of the toilet paper roll.

- Spot clean outside cabinets with warm water/dishsoap solution and cloth.

- Empty trash receptacle (often located next to toilet or under sink).

- Neatly fold any towels.

- Vacuum floor

- Hand clean floors (solution of tsp. of dishsoap or all-purpose/stone concentrate and warm water in bucket). DO NOT use excess water on wood floors. Only use damp rag or mop and wipe dry immediately after.

2. Kitchen

*Freely wipe all counters crumbs, etc onto floor, as you will vacuum later.

- Clean light fixtures with damp rag.

- Clean interior microwave with warm water/dishsoap (non-toxic) solution and scrub with non-abrasive sponge. Wipe clean with dry rag. Clean exterior with all-purpose spray or stainless steel cleaner.

- Place stove grates in sink; scrub with 1 tsp dishsoap and warm water solution. Rinse with water; dry with lint-free rag.

- Clean ceramic stovetop by spreading warm water/dishsoap solution on surface using a **magic eraser.** Let sit for 2 minutes; scrub, rinse and repeat. Wipe stove-top clean with dry, soft cloth.

- Spray stainless steel cleaner (or apply mineral oil) on exterior on all stainless steel appliances, including backsplash of stove, refrigerator, etc. Wipe with **soft cloth** *with* the direction of the surface's grain.

- Use granite cleaner or dishsoap and warm water and a soft cloth to clean granite.

- Clean outside of cupboards with 1 tsp dishsoap: 1 gallon warm water solution and soft cloth; wipe dry.

- Tie up garbage and recycling bags and take into appropriate area (i.e. garage). Replace with fresh bags provided by customer; wipe outside of can with all-purpose (or stainless steel) cleaner.

- Dry dust baseboards with cloth or vacuum with extension.

- Vacuum

- Spot clean stuck-on food on floors with damp rag.

- Damp mop kitchen floor with surface-appropriate product.

3. Living Areas

- Clean ceiling fan and light fixtures with damp

cloth.

- Dry dust blinds with microfiber cloth. If heavily soiled, use wet rag and wipe clean with dry towel.

- Carefully dust—top to bottom—accessible shelves, carefully cleaning underneath figurines.

- Dry dust T.V. stand, picture frames and other unfinished wood surfaces; use Pledge or Endust on all finished surfaces, including wood furniture, paneling, window ledges and more.

- Dry dust baseboards (if heavily soiled, wash).

- Fold blankets and place on couch or chair.

- Vacuum any carpet and/or wood floor, moving light furniture as needed.

- Damp mop floor with surface-appropriate product.

- Empty trash receptacle

Tip: If you are unsure of the type of floor surface you are working with, damp mop with water only, and use as little water as possible.

Chapter 5: My Biggest Mistakes

Here are two valuable lessons that I learned the hard way. Had I learned these principles before starting my cleaning service, I would have earned thousands of extra dollars in my first few years.

The first lesson I learned is related to Pareto's 80:20 principle, which states that for most events, 80% of the effects come from 20% of the causes. In regards to your cleaning service, this means that 20% of your top paying customers produce 80% of your revenue. Identify these top customers and make them your priority. Be more willing to follow up with referrals given to you by these customers, and always do your best work at these homes. Fire "bad customers" (i.e. one who cancels often or has an excessively dirty home) by referring them to another service nearby.

It is extremely easy in this industry to get bogged down and overwhelmed by every client's specific requests, instructions, favors, etc. *Learn to say no,* and don't worry about perfection. Your time in this business is everything. You will soon discover that there is far greater demand for good cleaning services than there are actual good services out there, thus giving you all of the negotiating power. Customers *need* you more than you need them. Your pricing should reflect this: unapologetically charge premium rates (we will get to pricing in a later chapter). If someone is unwilling to pay your rates, bid them farewell. This is especially important with a solo operation (a large cleaning service servicing a high number of accounts might be able to get away with some discounted pricing, but when it is just yourself, this can be crippling).

My problem early on was saying "yes" to virtually every customer's requests, and undercharging my services to quickly get my foot in the door. It took a couple of years to slowly increase my prices to get these early clients priced properly. In hindsight, this cost me thousands of dollars. Be assertive and confident from your business' inception, even if that means "faking it 'till you make it".

Tip: If you are feeling uneasy about charging high prices off the bat while you perfect your cleaning process, explain to your first few prospective customers that you are a new business and will offer them promotional pricing (10-20% off) for the first two cleanings while you work out the kinks. For the customer, this helps ease the concern of hiring a brand new service.

The second major lesson I learned the hard way surrounds Parkinson's law, which states "work expands so as to fill the time available for its completion." This means that it is *essential* to have strict time limits for each house you clean. Charge by the hour, and leave no questions as to quality standards. It's simple: if a customer wants something else cleaned or something cleaned deeper, they must pay for your time to do it. The scope of each cleaning depends on the amount of time they pay for, rather than your ability to complete the most tasks for a given flat rate.

I began by charging flat rates (big mistake). It left me questioning the quality and scope of each cleaning job. This caused me to spend *way* too much time at each job, getting caught up in the minutiae. **While the quality of the cleanings was great, I had set an unrealistic standard for my first few clients that I could not continue to meet as my business grew.** This forced me to abandon the flat-rate pricing model and switch to hourly pricing, which worked tremendously.

Tip: Parkinson 's law has an interesting effect on cleaning itself that you should use to your advantage. There is a reason we do our best work when facing a tight deadline (i.e. getting your best work done the night before an assignment is due). The same concept is true for cleaning. I often get more done in the final hour of cleaning a home than I do in the first two hours combined. Strict time limits for each cleaning session helps facilitate this enhanced productivity. Focus tightens, sense of time disappears (paradoxically) and we enter into what researchers call the flow state.

Chapter 6: Bonus Material

A. Making the work enjoyable

1. Audio podcasts allow you to absorb knowledge from some of the worlds brightest minds (on any topic you wish) for free while cleaning. The access to free information and entertainment on the job is empowering: you control the content of every minute on the job.

Tip: Wear headphones (for music and podcasts) to make the cleaning experience an immersive one.

2. Treat cleaning as a workout. With all of the personal fitness tracking devices out there (i.e. Fitbit), it is easy to track your physical activity throughout a cleaning job, including the number of steps you take, average heart rate, calories burned, etc. Incentivize your workers with small bonuses when they reach certain milestones to help make the physical component of cleaning—which many see as grueling—more bearable. This approach can help celebrate and shed positive light on the physical component of cleaning, especially when compared to a sedentary office lifestyle.

B. Cleaning Tips

A few gems…

1. Scrub shower door with damp magic eraser. Squeegee door top-to-bottom until clean.

2. To make a simple, eco friendly all-purpose

cleaner safe on most surfaces, mix water with a drop of dishsoap in empty spray bottle.

3. Cut up old pillow cases to convert to non-abrasive cleaning towels.

4. An eco-friendly alternative to normal stainless steel cleaner is mineral oil. Put a dab on soft cloth and wipe clean with the grain.

5. Carry extra vacuum belts and bags (if needed) in your car.

6. Leave a personalized thank you note after each cleaning.

7. Buy a lightweight stepstool for reaching high cabinets and ceiling fans.

8. Cut apart old pillowcases and towels to convert to "cleaning rags."

9. Utilize "wait time" of most cleaning agents— avoid prolonged bleach contact with surfaces, however.

10. Get gunk off your window by first dampening soiled area and then, using caution, scrape straightedge razor in one direction. Do not scrub.

Miscellaneous

1. Screen cleaning

Use a damp magic eraser on window screens then rinse. Use warm water with a drop of dishsoap.

2. Refrigerator/ freezer

Spray all-purpose cleaner on soiled areas. Wait 2 minutes, scrub with damp magic eraser, wipe clean with towel.

3. Blinds

Use a damp magic eraser to scrub soiled blinds. Wipe clean with dry rag. Use a microfiber cloth or feather duster to dry dust blinds.

4. Cleaning pet hair off couches:

- Use a lint roller
- Wet a finger of a rubber latex glove, run in circular motion over pet hair embedded in fabric of couch.
- Run a rubber squeegee over soiled areas

5. Wood floor care

- First, vacuum or sweep the floor entirely.
- Make a solution of ¼ cup white distilled vinegar and 1 gallon of warm water in a bucket. Use a microfiber damp mop pad to clean floors as an alternative to the water intensive mop and bucket. Rinse the pad as needed in your bucket; wring out well. Change your water frequently.
- NEVER use too much water on wood floors as floor boards will warp over time.
- Always clean *with* the grain of the wood.
- If you are unsure of the floor's finish, ask your customer what product their manufacturer

recommended during installation.

Note: damp mop only, as you are cleaning the finish, not the wood itself. Wet mopping warps floorboards over time, requiring costly replacement.

6. Cleaning marble/stone floors

Damp mop with soft pad/ warm water. Use a drop of dishsoap only when heavily soiled. Always rinse. Use stone cleaner periodically—excessive use can eat through the sealant and damage the actual stone itself.

7. Shower/bath

Mr. Clean Magic Erasers (or any generic form) are your best friend. Scrub (then squeegee) shower doors, porcelain tubs, sinks, even chrome. Use a scrubbing pad when necessary, but test in an inconspicuous area for scratching.

8. Vacuums

Invest in a Hoover Commercial Backpack Vacuum or a quality canister vacuum for use on wood and tile floors, baseboards, and even pet hair on couches/people hair found in bathrooms. This tool is crucial when faced with a heavily soiled rental unit. Be mindful, however, of the backpack vacuum's protruding design that makes knocking lamps and figurines over a risk.

9. Unfinished wood furniture

Dry dust all unfinished pieces. Use a dab of water (quickly drying it after) to loosen any stuck-on dirt.

C. Other

1. Phone Script

Answer by first identifying your company name, followed by your name.

Example: "Perfect Clean, this is Sheri."

Be ready to explain the services you offer, your pricing structure, and your availability for a service date or in-house estimate. Once a potential customer expresses interest in cleaning, take charge of the conservation by asking:

"Great—are you interested in regular service or a one-time clean?"

If a customer wishes to schedule, make sure you ask for and document the following:

- Customer name
- Describe your billing policy.
- House address/city (or apartment number and address)
- #bedrooms, bathrooms, approximate square footage of residence
- Ask your new customer if they have any

product preferences (especially when it comes to hardwood floor care) or any other special instructions for you or your workers.

- Ask if they will be home to let you in (if not, arrangements will have to be made to leave a key, share a temporary garage code, etc).

- Tell them about your cancellation policy, if one exists.

Before wrapping up the phone call, let your customer know of the best way to reach you if any questions come up prior to cleaning. Ask if they would like an appointment reminder via email or text (if so, collect customer's email).

2. Cleaning Preparation

To make optimal use of hired cleaning time, a few preparations by the homeowner beforehand can go a long way.

Here are some suggestions to help create a streamlined work environment, benefiting both cleaner and customer. Ask clients to:

- clear sink of dishes

- pick up items (toys, laundry, shoes, etc) from floor

- leave supplies on kitchen counter (i.e. toiletries to be restocked) with any specially preferred cleaning products.

- leave vacuum out for use, if they have one

- create space: most professional cleaners are used to working at empty homes with free reign of the house

- put away and account for any valuables

- secure all pets in cage or penned off area (unless addressed with designated cleaner beforehand)

3. Wrapping Up

When you are wrapping up a cleaning job, a few extra steps can go a long way in solidifying your service's value. Set yourself apart from other cleaning services in your area by going the extra mile.

Some ideas include:

- Leave a thank you note after each cleaning with any notes and the date/time of the next scheduled appointment.

- Bring any garbage cans up, if it is trash day.

- Quickly sweep out garage floor.

- Clean any noticeably soiled windows, including sliding doors with paw prints, and window over kitchen sink.

- Replenish garbage bags and toilet paper rolls. Empty trash receptacles in bathrooms and bedrooms.

- Fold blankets/towels and arrange remote controls nicely.

- Scrub kitchen sink clean; dry. Deodorize sink by pouring a half cup of distilled white vinegar down drain and letting sit.

- Wash any dog trays (for water/food bowls) and shoe mats; arrange shoes in orderly fashion.

- Scan the house for any cleaning products or rags your crew may have left behind.

Tip: the finishing touches of a job show your customer your willingness to go the extra mile, and could determine whether or not they will refer your service to friends and family in the area. Do not hurry when leaving!

Chapter 6: Cleaning Quiz (50 Questions)

Each answer is located at the bottom right of each question.

1. What is the most effective way to clean windows?

  a. Scrubber, squeegee and water

  b. Rag and Windex

  c. Newspaper and Windex

a.

2. True or False:

Water and vinegar should be used to clean finished marble floors.

False

3. The vacuum stopped spinning. This is most likely caused by:

  a. A loose screw

  b. Electrical malfunction

  c. A broken belt

c.

4. True or False:

Clean stainless steel *with* the grain.

True

5. Use the following natural product to clean stainless steel appliances:

a. Baby lotion

b. Mineral oil

c. White vinegar

b.

6. Clean windows:

a. In direct sunlight

b. While it's raining

c. In the shade

c.

7. What can damage laminate (artificial wood) flooring?

a. Too much water

b. Baking soda

c. Dishsoap

a.

8. What tool can clean both wall scuffs and

shower doors?

    a. Microfiber cloth

    b. Magic eraser

    c. Lemon oil

                                               b.

9. Microfiber cloths are most effective when:

    a. Wet

    b. Dry

    c. Soaked

                                               b.

10. To get rid of musty odors in your washing machine, add ½ cup of the following to your next load:

    a. White vinegar

    b. Dishsoap

    c. Ammonia

                                             a.

11. Scrub away years of buildup from baking sheets by:

    a. Scrubbing with equal parts hydrogen peroxide and baking soda

b. Leaving in the sun for a day

c. Using dishsoap and a sponge

a.

12. Remove oil stains from garage floors by scrubbing with:

a. White vinegar

b. Cola

c. Bleach

b.

13. Prevent soap scum buildup on shower doors by applying a thin layer of:

a. Olive oil

b. Shampoo

c. Lemon oil

c.

14. For efficiency, vacuum wood floors with:

a. Backpack vacuum or canister vacuum with soft brush attachment

b. Upright vacuum with rotating brush roll

c. Broom and dustpan

a.

15. Remove gunk stuck on your windows with:

    a. Abrasive side of sponge

    b. Scrubbing brush

    c. Wet straight-edge razor

                                            c.

16. If unsure whether a wood piece is finished or not, simply:

    a. Dry dust with soft cloth

    b. Use furniture polish and dry

    c. Use water only

                                            a.

17. Clean baseboards with _____ to remove static and help repel future dust from sticking.

    a. Socks

    b. Plastic bags

    c. Dryer sheets

                                            c.

18. Clean most coffee makers by brewing a mixture of:

    a. 1:2 parts water and baking soda

b. 1:1 parts water and white distilled vinegar

c. 1:1 parts red wine and coffee

b.

19. Restore scuffs on leather couches using:

a. Lemon oil

b. Shoe polish

c. Baking soda

b.

20. Never let the following cleaning product come into contact with your bathroom faucet fixtures:

a. Vinegar

b. Pine Sol

c. Bleach

c.

21. No garbage disposal? Keep your sink fresh by:

a. Pouring a pot of boiling water down sink

b. Pouring bleach down sink

c. Pouring lemon juice down sink

a.

22. Prevent soap scum buildup on porcelain bathtubs by applying a layer of:

a. Lemon oil

b. Car wax

c. Orange oil

b.

23. Clean foul smelling stains (i.e. feces) on carpet with:

a. Cold water

b. Hot water

c. Steam

a.

24. Clean blood stains on carpet using:

a. Vodka

b. Baking soda

c. Dishsoap and cold water

c.

25. Clean urine stains on carpet using:

a. White wine and water

b. White vinegar

c. Warm water, dishsoap, and white vinegar

c.

26. Clean oil/grease stains on carpet using:

a. All-purpose cleaner

b. Baking powder

c. Baking soda, water and scrub brush

c.

27. Clean red wine stains on carpet using:

a. Mild detergent and white vinegar/water

b. Baking soda

c. Hydrogen peroxide and water

a.

28. True or false: when spot cleaning spills on carpet, always blot affected area, never rub.

True

29. Clean hardened candle wax off carpet using:

a. Scrub brush and club soda

b. Scissors and baking soda

c. Clothing iron, cloth and knife

c.

30. Which household item is a natural deodorizer?

    a. Baking soda

    b. Lime

    c. Flour

a.

31. Which of the following household items are machine washable?

    a. Stuffed animals

    b. Shower curtains

    c. Both

c.

32. To loosen stuck-on gunk from your microwave, heat ½ cup of the following (in microwave-safe bowl) to a boil:

    a. Lemon water

    b. Club soda

    c. White vinegar

c.

33. Clean white grout with:

   a. Grout brush and ammonia

   b. Grout brush and bleaching agent

   c. Grout brush and coarse salt

b.

34. To prevent future stains, seal clean grout with:

   a. Caulk

   b. Paint sealer

   c. Masonry sealer

c.

35. Which of the following makes the best kitchen degreaser?

   a. Plant-based cleaners

   b. Citrus-based cleaners (i.e. orange oil)

   c. Acidic cleaners (i.e. white vinegar)

b.

36. Probiotic cleaners:

   a. Eliminate biofilm and other bad bacteria without harming healthy bacteria

   b. Are ideal for removing stubborn soap scum

without scrubbing

c. Should be used to clean toilets only

a.

37. Besides cleaning windows, what other handy uses do rubber squeegees provide?

a. Removing pet hair from carpet and rugs

b. Cleaning shower doors

c. Both

c.

38. Hard water deposits should be cleaned using:

a. An acidic cleaner

b. A basic cleaner

c. Baking soda

a.

39. NEVER mix the following two cleaning solutions:

a. Dishsoap and white vinegar

b. Bleach and baking soda

c. Bleach and ammonia-based products

c.

40. Clean rings from your toilet bowl with:

    a. Pumice stone

    b. Straight edge razor

    c. Sponge

                                            c.

41. Clean gum from wood by applying _____to the affected area, then use a dull knife to remove.

    a. Heat

    b. Water

    c. Ice

                                            c.

42. The safest way to clean sealed marble and granite floors:

    a. White vinegar and water

    b. Ammonia and water

    c. Dishsoap and water

                                            c.

43. What area in your home has the highest bacteria count?

    a. Stove

b. Toilet

c. Kitchen sink

c.

44. Turbo-charge your grease cleaning efforts in the kitchen by:

a. Heating damp sponge in microwave before applying degreaser

b. Turning up the thermostat 5-10 degrees

c. Opening up windows to ventilate area

a.

45. Use _____ to dust lampshades.

a. Duct tape

b. Scotch tape

c. Lint roller

c.

46. Clean heavily soiled (non-wooden) blinds by:

a. Spraying bleach and letting sit

b. Using cold water and lemon oil

c. Soaking in tub and scrubbing with all-purpose cleaner

c.

47. What cleaning product is best for cleaning surfaces soiled with tar and nicotine?

    a. Ammonia

    b. Bleach

    c. White vinegar

                                        a.

48. Clean your dishwasher by running a normal cycle and adding ½ cup of:

    a. Bleach

    b. Ammonia

    c. White vinegar

                                        c.

49. Always clean from:

    a. Left to right

    b. Bottom to top

    c. Top to bottom

                                        c.

50. Which describes the safest way to clean finished wood floors?

    a. Damp mop with soft pad or cloth

b. Wet mop with soft mop

c. Wet wop and hand dry

a.

Answer Key

1.a

2.False

3.c

4.True

5.b

6.c

7.a

8.b

9.b

10.a

11.a

12.b

13.c

14.a

15.c

16.a

17.c

18.b

19.b

20.c

21.a

22.b

23.a

24.a

25.c

26.c

27.a

28.True

29.c

30.a

31.c

32.c

33.b

34.c

35.b

36.a

37.a

38.a

39.c

40.a

41.c

42.c

43.c

44.a

45.c

46.c

47.a

48.c

49.c

50.a

In Closing

Starting a cleaning business can be empowering and financially rewarding if you charge premium rates, be firm with customers, and harness the power of the internet. Stick to these principles to enjoy residual earning power that will kickstart—or be the primary source of—your entrepreneurial journey.

Links to online resources mentioned in this book:

Accounting

www.mileiq.com

www.shoeboxed.com

www.waveapps.com

Billing

www.paypal.com

www.square.com

www.pocketsuite.io

Domain name

www.godaddy.com

Form builders

www.form2go.com

www.wufoo.com

Logo

www.fiverr.com

Online business listings and review sites

Google Business

www.yelp.com

www.manta.com

www.angieslist.com

http://services.amazon.com/ (not mentioned in ebook)

Online newsletter

www.mailchimp.com

Third-party property platforms

www.Airbnb.com

www.Zillow.com

Scheduling

www.acuityscheduling.com

www.pocketsuite.io

Website building platforms

www.wix.com

www.squarespace.com

www.000WebHost.com

If you enjoyed this book, please consider leaving a review. Thank you! Also, feel free to use any copy in the sample newsletters and estimate request forms for your own personal use.

23050638R00049

Made in the USA
San Bernardino, CA
19 January 2019